The Bernard and Irene Schwartz Series on American Competitiveness

The United States and the WTO Dispute Settlement System

Robert Z. Lawrence

CSR NO. 25, MARCH 2007
COUNCIL ON FOREIGN RELATIONS

10576697

Founded in 1921, the Council on Foreign Relations is an independent, national membership organization and a nonpartisan center for scholars dedicated to producing and disseminating ideas so that individual and corporate members, as well as policymakers, journalists, students, and interested citizens in the United States and other countries, can better understand the world and the foreign policy choices facing the United States and other governments. The Council does this by convening meetings; conducting a wide-ranging Studies Program; publishing *Foreign Affairs*, the preeminent journal covering international affairs and U.S. foreign policy; maintaining a diverse membership; sponsoring Independent Task Forces and Special Reports; and providing up-to-date information about the world and U.S. foreign policy on the Council's website, CFR.org.

THE COUNCIL TAKES NO INSTITUTIONAL POSITION ON POLICY ISSUES AND HAS NO AFFILIATION WITH THE U.S. GOVERNMENT. ALL STATEMENTS OF FACT AND EXPRESSIONS OF OPINION CONTAINED IN ITS PUBLICATIONS ARE THE SOLE RESPONSIBILITY OF THE AUTHOR OR AUTHORS.

Council Special Reports (CSRs) are concise policy briefs, produced to provide a rapid response to a developing crisis or contribute to the public's understanding of current policy dilemmas. CSRs are written by individual authors—who may be Council fellows or acknowledged experts from outside the institution—in consultation with an advisory committee, and are intended to take sixty days or less from inception to publication. The committee serves as a sounding board and provides feedback on a draft report. It usually meets twice—once before a draft is written and once again when there is a draft for review; however, advisory committee members, unlike Task Force members, are not asked to sign off on the report or to otherwise endorse it. Once published, CSRs are posted on the Council's website, CFR.org.

Council Special Reports in the Bernard and Irene Schwartz Series on American Competitiveness explore challenges to the long-term health of the U.S. economy. In a globalizing world, the prosperity of American firms and workers is ever more directly affected by critical government policy choices in areas such as spending, taxation, trade, immigration, and intellectual property rights. The reports in the Bernard and Irene Schwartz series analyze the major issues affecting American economic competitiveness and help policymakers identify the concrete steps they can take to promote it.

For further information about the Council or this report, please write to the Council on Foreign Relations, 58 East 68th Street, New York, NY 10021, or call the Communications office at 212-434-9400. Visit our website, CFR.org.

To submit a letter in response to a Council Special Report for publication on our website, CFR.org, you may send an email to CSReditor@cfr.org. Alternatively, letters may be mailed to us at: Publications Department, Council on Foreign Relations, 58 East 68th Street, New York, NY 10021. Letters should include the writer's name, postal address, and daytime phone number. Letters may be edited for length and clarity, and may be published online. Please do not send attachments. All letters become the property of the Council on Foreign Relations and will not be returned. We regret that, owing to the volume of correspondence, we cannot respond to every letter.

CONTENTS

FOREWORD

The Doha negotiations have stalled since last summer, and, as the November elections in the United States highlighted, American advocates of economic nationalism are growing in strength. Nevertheless, Robert Lawrence makes a case for the effectiveness of the World Trade Organization (WTO), particularly its dispute settlement system, and the benefits that would accrue to the United States and others from improving its effectiveness. These benefits include expanding world trade and increasing support for an often beleaguered organization that is central to the conduct of world trade.

In this Council Special Report, Professor Lawrence addresses the critics of the dispute settlement mechanism—both those who think it should be tougher on countries that violate trade rules and those who think it is already so tough as to violate sovereignty. He points out the successes of the WTO since its creation in 1995 and argues that radical changes to the system are ill-advised. Lawrence nonetheless suggests several areas for reform, from steps that require multilateral negotiations, such as improving opportunities for nonstate actor participation in and enhancing transparency of the process, to changes the United States could make in its own behavior.

This Council Special Report is part of the Bernard and Irene Schwartz Series on American Competitiveness and was produced by the Council's Maurice R. Greenberg Center for Geoeconomic Studies. The Council and the center are grateful to the Bernard and Irene Schwartz Foundation for its support of this important project.

Richard N. Haass
President
Council on Foreign Relations
March 2007

ACKNOWLEDGMENTS

I am particularly grateful to members of the Advisory Committee, organized by the Council on Foreign Relations, under the chairmanship of Susan G. Esserman. The members were Kira M. Alvarez, Raj Bhala, Barry E. Carter, Steve Charnovitz, Christine A. Elder, Elliot J. Feldman, Mercedes C. Fitchett, Robert E. Herzstein, Gary C. Hufbauer, Theodore H. Moran, Marcus Noland, Christina R. Sevilla, Shanker A. Singham, Sidney Weintraub, and Phoebe L. Yang. In two meetings, they gave me extensive and extremely helpful comments on earlier drafts.

I am grateful to Douglas Holtz-Eakin, former director of the Maurice R. Greenberg Center for Geoeconomic Studies, for directing this project; to Benn Steil, the Council's director of international economics, for offering me the opportunity to write this CSR; and to James Bergman for his editing and comments on various drafts. Sebastian Mallaby, who succeeded Doug Holtz-Eakin as director of the center, contributed the final edit.

I also thank Council President Richard N. Haass and Director of Studies Gary Samore for their comments. For their efforts in the production and dissemination of this report, I would like to thank Patricia Dorff and Lia Norton in the Publications department, and Lisa Shields and Brittany Mariotti on the Communications team.

Finally, I would like to thank the Bernard and Irene Schwartz Foundation for its generous support of this project.

Robert Z. Lawrence

ACRONYMS AND ABBREVIATIONS

AB	Appellate Body
ADA	Antidumping Act
AoA	Agreement on Agriculture
CAP	Common Agricultural Policy
DSB	Dispute Settlement Body
DSU	Dispute Settlement Understanding
EC	European Commission
EPA	Environmental Protection Agency
GATT	General Agreement on Tariffs and Trade
GMO	genetically modified organism
MFN	most favored nation
SCM	Agreement on Subsidies and Countervailing Measures
SPS	Agreement on Sanitary and Phytosanitary Measures
TRIMS	Trade-Related Investment Measures
TRIPS	Trade-Related Aspects of Intellectual Property Rights
TRQ	tariff rate quota
VAT	value-added tax
WTO	World Trade Organization
USTR	Office of the U.S. Trade Representative

COUNCIL SPECIAL REPORT

INTRODUCTION

The United States likes to think of itself as a nation that abides by its treaties and commitments. Successive U.S. administrations have taken the obligations implied by international agreements seriously: They have opted out of parts of many agreements for fear that compliance would be contrary to U.S. interests, and have refused outright to sign some treaties on the grounds of potential legal exposure. But U.S. behavior toward the World Trade Organization is different; in this case, the United States has been quite willing to accept binding multilateral rules. Yet, the United States has also been repeatedly judged to be in violation of its WTO commitments by the organization's dispute settlement panels, and although some violations could be ascribed to uncertainties about the meaning of the rules, the United States is also guilty of disregarding the rules deliberately. Opinion in Congress sometimes encourages this behavior; legislators are less likely to question the legitimacy of U.S. conduct than to question the WTO's authority to pass judgment over the United States. Moreover, these tensions are likely to escalate if the Doha Round of global trade negotiations breaks down. If the diplomatic route to market access is blocked, trading partners will seek access to U.S. consumers by bringing more cases before the WTO's tribunals. A surge in such cases could increase resentment of the WTO in the United States, weakening America's commitment to its traditional postwar role as the bulwark of the international trading system. This would be unfortunate, because even without changes in the behavior of its trading partners, the rules of the WTO improve the performance of the U.S. economy.

U.S. ambivalence toward the WTO starts with an ambivalence toward trade, and particularly with a misunderstanding of the sources of trade's benefits. The American public is quick to grasp the importance of exports, but the gains from trade go well beyond that. Exporting raises the prices producers can charge for their products and allows for economies of scale. Importing reduces product prices and increases the choices available to consumers. Trade also intensifies competition, thereby encouraging firms to be more productive and innovative. So despite the recent fracturing of the political consensus in favor of trade, the substantive case for it is accepted by just about every mainstream economist. According to one recent estimate, U.S. incomes are some 10 percent higher than they would be if the economy were self-sufficient.[1]

But trade cannot deliver prosperity in a vacuum. In a world of nation-states, moving goods and services across borders may require dealing with a host of institutional, regulatory, linguistic, legal, cultural, informational, and political factors.[2] International commerce is therefore more risky and associated with higher transaction costs than domestic commerce. The existence of rules, and a mechanism for enforcing them, is crucial to reducing these transaction costs. Firms sinking large investments in distribution and production need to be sure about the conditions that govern market access and the regulatory and competitive environments in which they will operate. Absent that certainty, the full potential of global engagement will not be realized.

Paradoxically, enforceable trade rules are important for the same reason that they are unpopular. Because trade creates winners and losers, there is always political pressure to disrupt trade even though its effect on the economy as a whole is positive. Under competitive conditions, imports provide consumers with benefits in excess of the costs to domestic producers, but producers often have more political influence. Similarly, international competition pits firms and workers from different nations against one another and leads to pressures for national political leaders to assist local producers at the expense of foreigners. National producers' pleas for help will be particularly hard to resist if they can argue that their foreign competitors receive help from their governments. Under these circumstances, trade rules play a crucial role, both in restraining protective measures that may directly reduce consumer welfare and in helping to reassure investors and workers that the system is equitable.

At a time when the Doha Round of trade negotiations has stalled and public opinion polls register skepticism about trade, it is worth emphasizing the contribution of

---

[1] See Scott C. Bradford, Paul L.E. Grieco, and Gary Clyde Hufbauer, "The Payoff to America from Global Integration," in C. Fred Bergsten, ed., *The United States and the World Economy: Foreign Economic Policy for the Next Decade* (Washington, DC: Peterson Institute for International Economics, 2005). For an appraisal of the benefits of trade to the U.S. competitiveness, see Martin N. Baily and Robert Z. Lawrence, "Competitiveness and the Assessment of Trade Performance," in Michael Mussa, ed., *Festschrift for C. Fred Bergsten* (Washington, DC: Peterson Institute for International Economics, 2007).

[2] Indeed, there is an extensive economic literature measuring the extent of so-called border effects, i.e., the many obstacles that lead to domestic rather than international transactions. See, for example, Scott C. Bradford and Robert Z. Lawrence, *Has Globalization Gone Far Enough?* (Washington, DC: Peterson Institute for International Economics, 2004).

enforceable rules to the trading system's legitimacy. Policymakers in Washington often suggest that support for trade can be bolstered by the use of antidumping suits and other trade-restricting measures that supposedly punish foreigners who "cheat" in order to win U.S. markets. In this view, the WTO's dispute settlement tribunals damage political support for trade, since the panels have frequently ruled against the use of U.S. trade remedies. But this "safety valve" argument is shortsighted. The use of antidumping suits is a game that more than one nation can play: In the absence of the WTO's dispute settlement tribunals, U.S. trading partners would obstruct U.S. exports by resorting to their own "fair-trade" measures, and U.S. resentment of the trading system would be heightened. Enforceable rules offer the best hope of forestalling a tit-for-tat use of protective barriers that would further contribute to the deterioration of support for trade. In sum, and contrary to what many policymakers suppose, vigorous dispute settlement tribunals make the revival of the Doha Round more likely.

The importance of enforceable multilateral rules is evident from the era in which they were absent. The lack of agreed-upon enforcement procedures under the original treaty of the postwar trading system—the General Agreement on Tariffs and Trade (GATT)—engendered considerable U.S. frustration. There were innumerable bilateral conflicts with the European Union over its Common Agricultural Policy (CAP) and with Japan over its closed market. These were extremely difficult to resolve. In response, the United States implemented laws such as Section 301 of the Trade Act of 1974 and the Super 301 provisions of the Omnibus Trade and Competitiveness Act of 1988. These provisions sought to remove "unreasonable and unjustifiable" barriers to U.S. exports by threatening unilateral trade sanctions.[3] While these measures met with mixed results, they did help convince other countries of the merits of establishing a more effective system at the WTO, which was created to succeed GATT in 1995.[4]

---

[3] For more on these provisions and their limitations, see Thomas O. Bayard and Kimberly Ann Elliot, *Reciprocity and Retaliation in U.S. Trade Policy* (Washington, DC: Peterson Institute for International Economics, 1994). Several of the disputes between the United States and the EU have gone on for decades. For a review, see Robert Z. Lawrence, *Crimes and Punishments? Retaliation under the WTO* (Washington, DC: Peterson Institute for International Economics, 2003), Chapter 4.

[4] According to Robert Hudec, "The United States had apparently made a convincing case that the U.S. Congress would continue to insist upon its new, bellicose, 'take-the-law into your own hands' legal policy unless and until GATT had a legal enforcement procedure that met U.S. standards of effectiveness. Governments who preferred a more cautious, more voluntary adjudication system had apparently persuaded themselves that the risk of unchecked U.S. legal aggression was a greater danger than an excessively

The WTO provides more benefits to the United States than GATT did. Its provisions cover more issues that are of interest to the United States: The WTO includes rules on standards and technical barriers to trade; it protects intellectual property; it covers agriculture and services. But the biggest advantage of the WTO is that it includes a mechanism to enforce these rules: the dispute settlement system. This has reduced the need for the United States to resort to unilateral retaliatory measures, limiting an important source of tension between the United States and its partners and so generating a significant foreign-policy dividend. Indeed, it is striking that since the advent of the dispute settlement system, the United States has generally abided by its agreement not to impose unilateral trade sanctions against WTO members without WTO authorization.[5] Naturally, the system has not been able to solve all the disputes that have arisen. But it has at least been able to contain the effects of these disputes. By authorizing retaliation but limiting its size, the WTO helps to prevent conflicts in which both parties and the trade system as a whole could be severely damaged.

The shift from bilateral to multilateral enforcement helps secure the legitimacy of the trading system and reduces the political costs associated with bilateral dispute settlement. It helps the United States itself keep protectionist impulses at bay. It is also particularly useful for dealing with disputes with America's largest trading partners, such as the European Union, Japan, China, India, and Brazil, with which the United States has not signed free trade agreements. And yet, despite these considerable strengths, support for the WTO and its dispute settlement system remains fragile. This report describes how that system operates, considers the arguments of its critics, and finally provides some recommendations for improvement.

---

demanding GATT legal system." Robert Hudec, *Enforcing International Trade Law* (Salem, NH: Butterworth Legal Publishers, 1993), p. 237.

[5] The controversial Bananas case, in which the United States initiated Section 301 proceedings against the EU in 1994 and 1995 before requesting a WTO panel in 1996, is an exception.

THE DISPUTE SETTLEMENT SYSTEM

According to the Dispute Settlement Understanding (DSU), the agreement establishing the dispute settlement system that was negotiated as part of the Uruguay Round of 1995, WTO members may seek to resolve conflicts through the good offices of the organization's director-general or by agreeing to arbitration; they may also invoke the formal dispute settlement mechanism. To pursue this last option, the parties in the dispute are first required to engage in consultation. If these consultations are unsatisfactory, a complainant can, within sixty days, request the establishment of a panel of three members to hear the case. The panel issues an interim report and then a final one. If it finds that a member has failed to comply, and that member does not appeal, the body can make a recommendation as to how the member could come into compliance. If it is impractical to comply immediately, the member is given "a reasonable period of time in which to do so."[6] The finding can also be appealed to a second panel of three members of a permanent seven-person Appellate Body (AB), which operates like the supreme court of the organization.

If the member loses the appeal and fails to act within a reasonable period of time, the rules call for the parties to negotiate compensation, "pending full implementation."[7] "Compensation" is generally understood to require the defendant to provide additional concessions, typically in the form of reducing other trade barriers of interest to the plaintiff. Compensation is, however, "voluntary"—and rare.[8] If after twenty days, compensation cannot be agreed upon, the complainant may request authorization to suspend equivalent concessions. In particular, "the level of the suspension of concession … shall be equivalent to the level of nullification and impairment."[9] When, for example, the WTO found that the EU had cost the United States $116.8 million worth of exports by illegally banning hormone-fed beef, the United States was authorized to impose

---

[6] World Trade Organization, "Understanding on Rules and Procedures Governing the Settlement of Disputes," Annex 2 to the *Agreement Establishing the World Trade Organization*, Art. 21.3.
[7] Ibid., Art. 22.2.
[8] Ibid., Art. 22.1, which states, "compensation is voluntary and, if granted, shall be consistent with the covered agreements." This is generally understood to require that it be based on most-favored-nation (MFN) principles.
[9] Ibid., Art. 22.4.

punitive tariffs on $116.8 million worth of EU exports.[10] Arbitration, to be completed within sixty days, may be sought on the level of suspension, the procedures, and the principles of retaliation.[11]

The dispute settlement system has generally been successful in helping members resolve disputes and in obtaining compliance where violations have been found. Many cases have been settled in the consultation stage.[12] While there are delays, particularly when legislative action is required, and a few cases in which compliance has been lacking, the evidence suggests that by and large the United States and other countries eventually come into compliance.[13] Nations appear to comply less because of retaliation, which has rarely been used, but rather because they believe it is in their interest to do so.[14] This is because on balance they benefit from the rules and care about their reputations in a system in which there are ongoing negotiations. They also care about their relationships with significant trading partners.[15]

The system has been used extensively by the United States, but the United States has not dominated it. Table 1 (see Appendixes) provides a listing of several cases the United States has launched successfully. It illustrates how the United States has been able to challenge foreign measures that have inhibited U.S. exports through discriminatory

---

[10] See Charan Devereaux, Robert Z. Lawrence, and Michael D. Watkins, *Case Studies in US Trade Negotiation, Volume 2: Resolving Disputes* (Washington, DC: Institute for International Economics, 2006), p. 72.

[11] "Dispute Settlement Understanding," Art. 22.6.

[12] For an analysis see Marc L. Busch and Eric Reinhardt, "Developing Countries and General Agreement on Tariffs and Trade/World Trade Organization Dispute Settlement," *Journal of World Trade*, Vol. 37, No. 4 (2003), pp. 719–35.

[13] The case between the United States and the EU regarding hormone-fed beef is one example. For a detailed discussion see Devereaux, *Case Studies in US Trade Negotiation*, Chapter 1; and Benjamin L. Brimeyer, "Bananas, Beef and Compliance in the World Trade Organization: The Inability of the WTO Dispute Settlement Process to Achieve Compliance from Superpower Nations," *Minnesota Journal of Global Trade*, Vol. 10, No. 1 (2001), p. 133. William F. Davey, in "The WTO Dispute Settlement System: The First Ten Years," *Journal of International Economic Law*, Vol. 8, No. 1 (2005), pp. 17–50, found there was compliance in 83 percent of the 181 WTO cases prior to June 2002. Similarly high rates were found under GATT by Robert Hudec in *Enforcing International Trade Law*.

[14] Fabien Besson and Racem Mehdi do not find support for the hypothesis that retaliation significantly hampers developing countries' effectiveness in DSU. See Fabien Besson and Racem Mehdi, "Is the WTO Dispute Settlement System Biased Against Developing Countries? An Empirical Analysis," paper presented at the Second International Conference on "European and International Political & Economic Affairs," Athens, Greece, May 27–29, 2004.

[15] Chad Bown finds that, the more trade between disputants, the greater the compliance. He interprets this as evidence that retaliation is important in inducing compliance, but since retaliation is rare, it indicates only that compliance is enhanced by extensive trade relations. See Chad P. Bown, "On the Economic Success of GATT/WTO Dispute Settlement," *The Review of Economics and Statistics*, Vol. 86, No. 3 (2004), pp. 811–23.

taxes (e.g., Chinese value-added tax [VAT] rebates on domestic semiconductors), nontariff barriers (e.g., Indian quotas), inappropriate regulations (e.g., Japanese apples), unfair applications of the trade laws (e.g., Mexican antidumping and countervailing duties), and failure to protect intellectual property (e.g., the Pakistani patent regime and Japanese copyright rules). Table 2, by contrast, reports cases filed against the United States. These losses assist the U.S. government in avoiding protectionist and discriminatory measures and regulations. These include U.S. steel safeguards, U.S. antidumping practices (Byrd Amendment), export subsidies (Foreign Sales Corporation), regulatory practices that discriminated against foreigners (Venezuela and Brazilian petroleum refiners), and cotton subsidies (Brazil).

Although the very least developed countries do experience difficulties in using the system, there is evidence that it is being widely used by both developed and developing countries in rough proportion to their shares in world trade.[16] Between 1995 and 2000, for example, high-income countries filed 70.2 percent of disputes, while developing countries represented 29.8 percent of submitted cases. In the next five years (2001–2006), by contrast, developing countries filed a majority of the cases brought (52.1 percent).[17] While these numbers reflect mainly developing countries with large export shares, such as India and Brazil, there are also cases of small developing countries that have leveraged

---

[16] On the difficulties experienced by least developed countries, see Andrew T. Guzman and Beth Simmons, "Power Plays and Capacity Constraints: The Selection of Defendants in WTO Disputes," paper presented at the University of Wisconsin, 2005. There is, however, also evidence that the very least developed countries have trouble participating because of a lack of resources and expertise. See Chad P. Bown and Bernard Hoekman, "WTO Dispute Settlement and the Missing Developing Country Cases: Engaging the Private Sector," *Journal of International Economic Law*, Vol. 8, No. 4 (2005), pp. 861–90; Chad P. Bown, "Developing Countries as Plaintiffs and Defendants in GATT/WTO Trade Disputes," *The World Economy*, Vol. 27, No. 1 (2004), pp. 59–80; Besson and Mehdi, "Is the WTO Dispute Settlement System Biased Against Developing Countries?"; Busch and Reinhardt, "Developing Countries and General Agreement on Tariffs and Trade/World Trade Organization Dispute Settlement"; Gregory Schaffer, "Weaknesses and Proposed Improvements to the WTO Dispute Settlement System: An Economic and Market Oriented View," paper prepared for "WTO at 10: A Look at the Appellate Body," Sao Paulo, May 16–17, 2005; and Victor Mosoti, "Africa in the First Decade of WTO Dispute Settlement," *Journal of International Economic Law*, Vol. 9, No. 2 (2006), pp. 427–53. Political considerations, e.g., aid withdrawal and concern for revocation of the Generalized System of Preferences, are said to inhibit developing countries' effective use of the DSU, according to Chad P. Bown in "Participation in WTO Dispute Settlement: Complainants, Interested Parties and Free Riders," *World Bank Economic Review*, Vol. 19, No. 2 (2005), pp. 287–310; and William J. Davey "The WTO Dispute Settlement System: How Have Developing Countries Fared?" *Illinois Public Law and Legal Theory Research Paper*, No. 05-17 (2005).
[17] Figures calculated from http://www.worldtradelaw.net.

the system effectively to challenge large trading partners.[18] Another noticeable development is the increase in South-South disputes.[19] All in all, recent trends attest to developing countries' increased knowledge of and confidence in the WTO dispute resolution process.

Several features of the system merit emphasis. First, the WTO itself does not conduct investigations and instigate proceedings. Although the WTO does review its members' trade policies, there is no central policing mechanism—enforcement is carried out entirely as a result of member initiatives. While the respondents cannot block the case from going forward, the claimant may withdraw the case at any time, even if the defendant has not come into compliance.

Second, the operation of the system reflects the nature of the WTO as an *intergovernmental* organization.[20] Although private counsel can be employed to make arguments, and amicus briefs by nongovernmental entities have been allowed on occasion, only governments have standing to bring cases.[21] There is no private right of action. Violations of the agreements may have damaged private parties, but they have no recourse on their own and must operate through their governments. Similarly, retaliation is undertaken against the defendant country, and it could inflict damage on the incomes of exporting firms that had nothing to do with the infraction and whose only error was being located in the defending country—a reason why some believe that only compensation should be allowed.

---

[18] For example, Costa Rica against the United States concerning bans on the imports of cotton and fiber underwear in 1995; Antigua and Barbuda against the United States concerning cross-border supply of Internet gambling and betting in 2003; and Bangladesh, a least developed country (LDC), against India in antidumping measures in 2004.

[19] See OECD, "Analysis of Nontariff Barriers of Concern to Developing Countries," in *OECD Trade Policy Working Papers*, No. 16 (OECD Publishing, 2005). It is also interesting to note that, according to the OECD, South-South cases increasingly resemble what used to be thought of as North-South disputes: for instance, antidumping and sanitary and phytosanitary measures.

[20] With an important recent exception concerning EU compliance in the beef-hormone case, panel proceedings have occurred in closed sessions with only the participants in the dispute in attendance.

[21] *Banana III: European Communities—Regimes for the Importation, Sale and Distribution of Bananas* allowed member states to employ private lawyers in their litigation, and the turtle-shrimp and asbestos cases opened up the process to amici briefs. See World Trade Organization Appellate Body, *European Communities—Regimes for the Importation, Sale and Distribution of Bananas*, AB-1997-3, WT/DS27/AB/R, September 9, 1997.

Third, the DSU does not ordain a common law system with binding precedents. Technically, there is no stare decisis.[22] Each panel ruling is thus in principle unique—only the members themselves can adopt rules that "add to or diminish the rights and obligations" in the agreement.[23] In practice, however, precedents are actually given great weight, and panel and Appellate Body reports refer frequently and deferentially in many footnotes to the reasoning contained in other reports. The Appellate Body plays a particularly important oversight role in disciplining judgments and ensuring their consistency. Thus, de facto, the DSU has established something approaching a common-law system.

Fourth, WTO rulings are not automatically implemented. In practice, even if not technically in law, members have discretion as to whether they will comply; they may refuse even though this may mean breaking the agreement and perhaps facing retaliation against their exports. De jure such retaliation is meant to be temporary and is not a substitute for compliance.[24] But de facto retaliation can become the permanent outcome of a dispute. This means that the retaliation system may operate as a safety valve.

Fifth, there is no attempt to compensate the winner for damages incurred during the period of noncompliance, a practice that stands in contrast to contract cases in common-law legal systems. This has the advantage of not generating further disputes over the size and payment of such damages. But the downside is that parties expecting to lose have an incentive to delay the process as long as possible. Parties also may engage in rule-breaking behavior in the knowledge that the most that they will have to do is come into compliance at a later date.

In sum, the WTO dispute settlement mechanism is a distinctive form of arbitration combined with a variation of judicial review. The parties are required to submit to the process if one party launches a complaint. An arbitration panel investigates

---

[22] See Raj Bhala, "The Power of the Past: Towards de Jure Stare Decisis in WTO Adjudication," *George Washington International Review*, Vol. 33, Nos. 3 and 4 (2001), pp. 873–978; "The Myth about Stare Decisis and International Trade Law," *American University International Law Review*, Vol. 12, No. 4 (1999), pp. 845–956; and "The Precedent Setters: De Facto Stare Decisis in WTO Adjudication," *Journal of Transnational Law and Policy*, Vol. 9, No. 1 (1999), pp. 1–151.

[23] "Dispute Settlement Understanding," Art. 3.2.

[24] See John H. Jackson, "The WTO Dispute Settlement Understanding: Misunderstandings on the Nature of Legal Obligations," *American Journal of International Law*, Vol. 91, No. 2 (1997), pp. 60–64; and "The Changing Fundamentals of International Law and Ten Years of the WTO," *Journal of International Economic Law*, Vol. 8, No. 1 (2005), pp. 3–15.

and reaches conclusions based on rules previously negotiated by the members. The resulting rulings are binding on the parties. Failure to comply or provide compensation can result in the suspension of concessions. The rulings are also subject to appeal. However, the WTO system remains weaker than the arbitration processes common in domestic legal systems for four major reasons: Enforcement is not automatic, precedents are not strictly binding, standing of all injured parties is not assured—only governments bring cases—and remedies are limited.

ADDRESSING THE CRITICS

Even though trade boosts growth, and even though predictable rules buttressed by a dispute settlement system are important in promoting trade, WTO panels are subject to two types of objection. The first is that participation in a multilateral institution such as the WTO results in a loss of sovereignty for the United States. The second is that the process of transforming the WTO into a quasi-legal body has gone too far, and that arbitration panels have too much power in interpreting the rules of the WTO, which are often deliberately broad or ambiguous.

LOSS OF SOVEREIGNTY?

The sovereignty concerns surrounding the WTO have been expressed by critics on both ends of the political spectrum. From the left, Ralph Nader has declared that "few people have considered what adoption of the Uruguay Round Agreement would mean to U.S. democracy, sovereignty and legislative prerogatives … decisions arising [from WTO] governance can pull down our higher living standards in key areas or impose fines and other sanctions until such degradation is accepted."[25] From the right, conservative critics have registered similar objections to the United States as a sovereign nation being subjected to international rules, adjudicatory verdicts, and alleged penalties imposed by foreign nations. According to this view, there are excessive costs from being subject to an international legal regime. By preventing the United States from pursuing policies that would allegedly be in its interest, the WTO could actually reduce living standards.

---

[25] Quoted in John H. Jackson, "Sovereignty, Subsidiarity, and Separation of Powers: The High-wire Balancing Act of Globalization," in Daniel L.M. Kennedy and James D. Southwick, eds., *The Political Economy of International Trade Law: Essays in Honor of Robert E. Hudec,* (New York, NY: Cambridge University Press, 2002), p. 18. WTO opponents such as Nader routinely describe WTO retaliation as fines. According to Nader, "Once the WTO's secret tribunals issue their edicts, no independent appeals are possible. Worldwide conformity or continued payment of fines is required" (Ibid.). See Lori Wallach and Michelle Sforza, *The WTO: Five Years of Reasons to Resist Corporate Globalization* (New York, NY: Seven Stories Press, 1999), p. 7.

To consider these objections, it is necessary to delve into the specific institutional characteristics of the system. The first point to note is that decision-making at the WTO is by consensus; this means there is no rule or provision that the United States has not voluntarily accepted. Unlike the UN General Assembly, and like the UN Security Council, the United States can, on its own, prevent agreement in the WTO. To be sure, having signed an agreement, the United States is then constrained to comply; but it is wrong to assert that it has abridged its sovereignty by agreeing to abide by WTO rules. After all, all meaningful treaties involve restraints on behavior, yet the act of signing a treaty reflects the exercise of sovereignty. As with any contract, in the WTO, the United States agrees to constrain its behavior in return for other countries agreeing to constrain theirs. Just as individuals do not lose their liberty when they voluntarily sign beneficial contracts, so nations do not abridge their sovereignty when they sign trade agreements that advance their interests.

Notwithstanding some of the claims of its critics to the contrary, the WTO system is extremely respectful of national sovereignty.[26] As noted, the WTO itself does not bring its members to task when they violate the rules. It relies on member states to bring disputes before it. In addition, as noted above, countries are presumed to act in good faith, and when found to be in violation, are required only to come into compliance and not to compensate retroactively for breaches they may have committed. Since WTO rulings are not implemented automatically, the United States itself has to change its laws or rules in the face of a violation. Thus the United States retains "ultimate legal authority," and it can refuse to comply. To be sure, a finding of violation could lead a foreign country to retaliate against U.S. exports, but these authorizations have been rare (only in Foreign Sales Corporation and Extraterritorial Income Exclusion, the 1916 Anti-Dumping Act, and the Byrd Amendment). And even in these instances, the United States has not been forced to change its laws. If the United States chooses, it can simply live with the retaliation without further consequence.

It is also incorrect to treat retaliation by another WTO member as if it were a fine or penalty. Indeed, the WTO agreements refer to retaliation, in neutral language, as "the

---

[26] See Jackson, "Sovereignty, Subsidiarity, and Separation of Powers."

suspension of concessions." In principle the WTO operates on the basis of reciprocity.[27] This means that in order to obtain market access from the United States originally, the claimant in the case made an equivalent market-opening concession. If the United States is found in violation, it means the United States did not carry out its part of the agreement. Thus when the claimant retaliates against the United States, it is not imposing a fine but simply suspending concessions that are equal to the impairment of the benefits it originally granted. The disputants are basically going back to square one: the state of affairs prior to the agreement.

Far from limiting U.S. sovereignty, this form of retaliation actually favors the United States. The United States has a very large market and its ability to grant concessions makes it unusually influential in a system in which agreements are based on reciprocity. The ability to retaliate also provides the United States and other countries that have large markets the greatest ability, first, to bargain in the shadow of the law, i.e., use the implicit threat of bringing cases to induce compliance from other countries; second, to enforce rulings against other countries in the event of noncompliance; and third, to withstand retaliation in the event that others are authorized to take action against it. While all WTO members are formally equal, the system's design gives some countries more power than others.

Of course, from the standpoint of smaller countries, the system is still viewed as unfair, and there have been numerous proposals to reduce the weight given to market size in the system's bargaining and enforcement. Some have suggested that retaliation should be undertaken multilaterally or even that the right to retaliate should be auctioned. [28] In other words, if country A is authorized to retaliate against country B because B has committed a violation, it should be allowed to sell the right to impose tariffs on B's exports to other countries. But these alternatives are problematic for an organization that seeks to promote free trade. In particular, multilateral retaliation might be infeasible if countries that are not involved in a dispute are unwilling to raise their trade barriers, and selling the rights to retaliate is incompatible with the central premise of the WTO that

---

[27] See Kyle Bagwell and Robert Staiger, *The Economics of the World Trading System* (Cambridge, MA: MIT Press, 2002).

[28] See Kyle Bagwell, Petros Mavroidis, and Robert Staiger, "The Case for Auctioning Countermeasures in the WTO," NBER Working Paper No. W 9920 (2003).

15

protection is undesirable and therefore not something a country should be willing to pay for.[29]

A second imbalance that puts the United States in an advantageous position is its experience in dealing with the dispute settlement system. Not only does it make extensive use of the system to bring cases, but (like the EU) it participates as an interested third party in nearly every case that is brought. Even though developing countries are gaining experience in using the system, they are unlikely ever to match the expertise that big countries can marshal.[30]

TOO MUCH RULE OF LAW?

In addition to concerns over sovereignty, there are also differences of emphasis on the precise nature of the WTO's legal order. As Article 3 of the DSU points out, the system has three basic functions: first, to promptly settle disputes; second, to preserve members' rights; and third, to clarify the meaning of the existing provisions.[31] There are obvious tensions among these goals, and they have engendered some controversy. In particular, the need to settle disputes decisively can at times conflict with the goal of respecting members' sovereignty. This is a long-standing conflict.[32] One way to frame it is as a conflict between the legal and diplomatic dimensions of the agreement.

---

[29] For a proposal to establish contingent liberalization commitments that would not have these defects, see Robert Z. Lawrence, *Crimes and Punishments?*

[30] See Chad P. Bown and Bernard Hoekman, "WTO Dispute Settlement and the Missing Developing Country Cases: Engaging the Private Sector," *Journal of International Economic Law*, Vol. 8, No. 4 (2005), pp. 861–90; and Besson and Mehdi, "Is the WTO Dispute Settlement System Biased Against Developing Countries?"

[31] "The dispute settlement system of the WTO is a central element in providing security and predictability to the multilateral trading system. The Members recognize that it serves to preserve the rights and obligations of Members under the covered agreements, and to clarify the existing provisions of those agreements in accordance with customary rules of interpretation of public international law. Recommendations and rulings of the DSB cannot add to or diminish the rights and obligations provided in the covered agreements" ("Dispute Settlement Understanding," Art. 3.2). "The prompt settlement of situations in which a Member considers that any benefits … are being impaired is essential to the effective functioning of the WTO" ("Dispute Settlement Understanding," Art. 3.3).

[32] Under GATT, "crafting outcomes that would command the consent of both parties and thus be adopted was the principal task of the panelists," according to J.H.H. Weiler, "The Rule of Lawyers and the Ethos of Diplomats: Reflections on WTO Dispute Settlement," in Roger B. Porter, et al., eds., *Efficiency, Equity, Legitimacy: The Multilateral Trading System at the Millennium* (Washington, DC: Brookings Institution, 2001), p. 338.

The dispute settlement mechanism has been criticized by members of both the legal and the diplomatic camp. The legal camp points to the merits of a trading system based on enforceable rules and contrasts it with a system based on power politics. Legal scholar John Jackson, for example, emphasizes the importance of such rules in establishing a predictable framework for private decisions. Proponents of this view stress the importance of compliance and are critical of notions that countries could escape their obligations by implementing side deals or simply accepting retaliation as a tolerable alternative to compliance. They also argue that the WTO's rules should be interpreted to allow for enforcement even in cases where violations have had no impact on trade flows.[33] Likewise, Petros Mavroidis has argued that retaliation under the WTO is insufficiently forceful, and has advocated the use of more punitive responses in the event of noncompliance.[34]

Meanwhile, the diplomatic camp levies the opposite criticism. It sees dangers in an excessive legalization of the process in one form or another. WTO agreements reflect the need to obtain a consensus and are often written with what can charitably be termed "diplomatic ambiguity." This may be a virtue when it comes to obtaining agreement, but it is problematic when it comes to interpreting it. Given this ambiguity, Claude Barfield and Marco Bronckers maintain that there is now a dangerous mismatch between the speed and efficiency with which the dispute settlement process acts and the lengthy delays associated with negotiating new rules. They fear that since the rules are often unclear, there could be excessive judicial activism on the part of the panels, which inevitably try to fill in the gaps and deal with the ambiguities created by negotiators. Such actions, they argue, could undermine national democratic decision-making and lead to rules written by panelists rather than agreed to by the United States. Barfield has

---

[33] Article 3.8 of the DSU states, "In cases where there is an infringement of the obligations assumed under a covered agreement, the action is considered *prima facie* to constitute a case of nullification and impairment. This means there is normally a presumption that a breach of the rules has had an adverse impact on other Members parties to that covered agreement, and in such cases, it shall be up to the Member against whom the complaint has been brought to rebut the charge." Jackson observes that "this makes the presumption of nullification and impairment derive *ipso facto* from a violation, thus almost discarding the nullification and impairment concept in favor of a focus on whether or not a 'violation' or 'breach' of obligation exists." John H. Jackson, "Dispute Settlement and the WTO: Emerging Problems," *Journal of International Economic Law*, Vol. 1, No. 3 (1998), p. 332.

[34] Petros C. Mavroidis, "Remedies in the WTO Legal System: Between a Rock and a Hard Place," *European Journal of International Law*, Vol. 11, No. 4 (2000), pp. 763–814.

therefore argued in favor of mechanisms for short-circuiting and/or blocking the dispute settlement process by providing for a political veto, possibly by the director-general.[35]

Others have offered variants on this proposal, partly out of a related concern that WTO panels could actually impede future trade liberalization by issuing rulings that go beyond those strictly necessary to resolve a dispute. It is important to remember that the WTO is a forum for negotiation of new agreements as well as a system for enforcement of existing ones. If countries fear that they could be punished severely for noncompliance, they will be reluctant to sign agreements in the first place. This concern led the U.S. and Chilean governments to jointly propose in the Doha Round negotiations that participants in a dispute be given the opportunity, where they agree, to edit the final version of any decisions.[36]

There are other reasons to be wary of an aggressive move toward tougher enforcement. Not only may ambiguity allow the dispute settlement panels too much room for interpretation; member states may also be genuinely uncertain as to the precise meaning of the agreement, and their violations might not be deliberate. In addition, circumstances change, and members could find that an agreement turns out to be far more costly than anticipated. Unfortunately, while there are provisions in the WTO for rescheduling tariff concessions and for safeguards in the event of unforeseen circumstances, there are no equivalent provisions for rescheduling rules.[37] Given this deficiency, there is a case for the system to have safety valves.[38] Alan Sykes and Warren Schwartz have undertaken an interesting analysis of the WTO system using the economic theory of contract remedies that argues that at times permitting breach may be desirable.[39] Compliance is certainly desirable in most cases, but it is important to remember that it

---

[35] See Claude E. Barfield, *Free Trade, Sovereignty, Democracy: The Future of the World Trade Organization* (Washington, DC: AEI Press, 2001), p. 13.

[36] They argued that "the reasoning and findings of a report may at times go beyond what the parties consider necessary to resolve the dispute, or in some circumstances may even be counterproductive to resolution of the dispute." See "On Improving Flexibility and Member Control in WTO Dispute Settlement," *Negotiations on Improvements and Clarifications of the Dispute Settlement Understanding*, contribution by Chile and the United States, p. 1.

[37] *General Agreement on Tariffs and Trade* (1994), Arts. XXVII and XIX.

[38] For a rigorous demonstration of the benefits from a safety valve, see B. Peter Rosendorf and Helen V. Milner, "The Optimal Design of International Trade Institutions: Uncertainty and Escape," *International Organization*, Vol. 55, No. 4 (2004), pp. 829–57.

[39] Warren F. Schwartz and Alan O. Sykes, "The Economic Structure of Renegotiation and Dispute Resolution in the WTO/GATT System," John M. Olin Law and Economics Working Paper No. 143 (2002).

may not always be preferable. The WTO is an agreement-regulating economic activity, and as with contracts there are times when breach may be efficient.

It is well recognized in economics that barriers to exit can create barriers to entry. Restrictions on firing workers, for example, can discourage firms from hiring workers. Similarly, severe penalties could discourage members from agreeing to WTO disciplines in the first place. This is important because one role of the WTO system is to entice the parties to sign as many agreements as possible. As Kenneth Dam noted in his classic study of GATT,

> The GATT has a special interest in seeing that as many agreements for the reduction of tariffs as possible are made. Enforcement of tariff bindings is important … but … a system that made the withdrawal of concessions impossible would tend to discourage the making of concessions in the first place. *It is better, for example, that 100 commitments should be made and that 10 should be withdrawn than that only 50 commitments should be made and all of them kept.* [40]

Retaliation provides an incentive for compliance, but because it is limited to the amount of nullification and impairment, it does not compel it at all costs. Wilfred Ethier has argued persuasively that rebalancing with commensurate responses is the optimal approach when countries negotiating trade agreements are subject to considerable uncertainty about whether or not they could find themselves out of compliance. "Each country knows that it might turn out to be either the accuser or the accused. Thus it is in no country's interest, ex ante, to agree that, ex post, either the accuser should be unconstrained in its ability to punish or the accused should be unconstrained in its ability to proceed without punishment."[41] The United States should take this insight to heart. By one reckoning, since the DSU was negotiated the United States has been a plaintiff in eighty-four cases and a defendant in ninety-four.

---

[40] Kenneth W. Dam, *The GATT: Law and International Economic Organization* (Chicago, IL: University of Chicago Press, 1970), p. 80, emphasis added.
[41] See Wilfred Ethier, *Punishments and Dispute Settlement in Trade Agreements* (Copenhagen: Economic Policy Research Unit, 2001), p. 5.

In sum, the dispute settlement system reflects a subtle amalgam of the legal and diplomatic approaches. It places the initiative to bring and settle cases with the members, not the organization. It brings nations to task when they violate the rules, yet at the same time it is respectful of their sovereignty. It has allowed the dispute settlement system to clarify the rules, yet constrained it to be deferential to the words of the agreement. It has effectively induced compliance in the face of most violations, yet in some cases it has also accommodated breach. It is important to be aware that there are dangers from upsetting this balance. The demands for reform from the legal and the diplomatic camps cancel each other out. Moving strongly now in one or another direction could well lead to outcomes that are inferior.

Consider some of the proposals reviewed in the last section. Moving in the direction of diplomatic circuit breakers could undermine the system's usefulness. Imagine the cries of foul if the director-general of the WTO (or a subset of WTO members) unilaterally made the decision that a dispute was too controversial or political, or that the language agreed upon by a consensus of WTO members was too vague for a dispute settlement panel to render a judgment. One can well imagine those who believe they have the upper hand in the dispute complaining vehemently that their rights were being overruled by an unrepresentative group of members or, even worse, a bureaucrat like the director-general of the WTO. Likewise, it is hard to imagine that a victorious litigant would look favorably at a decision being overruled by a blocking minority of members—Barfield's second recommendation. Adopting these suggestions might well reduce the WTO's legitimacy—the opposite of what WTO critics in the diplomatic camp contend—and they would certainly impair its efficacy. Alternatively, a sudden leap toward tougher enforcement of the sort advocated by the legal camp would be similarly unwise. Imagine the impact of trying to insist, at all costs, that the European Union open its markets to U.S. beef fed with hormones. Given the lack of faith on the part of many Europeans in their food regulatory systems, the political damage to the WTO's standing could far outweigh any gains from increased sales by the United States. It is at times better to have the lights go out due to an electric fuse than to have the house burn down.

PRESCRIPTIONS AND CONCLUSIONS

The current dispute settlement system provides the United States numerous benefits, but there are also steps it could take to increase these benefits. Some of these would require a change in the rules under which the system operates and would therefore have to be introduced as part of a multilateral round of negotiations, such as the current Doha Round, in which there is a group discussing dispute settlement reform; others would simply require a change in U.S. behavior.

CHANGES TO THE SYSTEM

Enhanced Participation and Transparency

When GATT dealt only with trade and had a weak dispute settlement system it was relatively uncontroversial, but this has not been the case with the WTO.[42] The combination of the increased scope of the rules and the more juridical nature of the dispute settlement system has made it more vulnerable to challenge on the grounds that it lacks political legitimacy and accountability. Multinational firms and nongovernmental institutions have considerable interests in the trading system's rules, but if they wish to be heard at the WTO, they must rely on national governments to represent them. It is not easy to deal with this problem when standards of accountability and legitimacy are set by democratic nation-states. Giving nongovernmental actors independent access could also be criticized as undemocratic since they are not chosen by representative bodies, and may give undue weight to particular interests or concerns, but the system should surely improve participation by giving non-state actors improved opportunities for their views to be heard. Currently, amicus briefs are allowed where the panels agree, but it would be

---

[42] See Robert Howse, and Kalypso Nicolaides, "Legitimacy and Global Governance: Why Constitutionalizaing the WTO Is a Step Too Far," in Roger Porter, et al., eds., *Efficiency, Equity, Legitimacy: The Multilateral Trading System at the Millennium* (Washington, DC: The Brookings Institution, 2001), pp. 227–49.

preferable if the DSU were amended to allow the submission of amicus briefs by interested parties in *all* cases.

Transparency can also help to bolster legitimacy and contribute to the dispute settlement system's role in informing private participants about WTO rules and issues. There is no reason why only participants in a case are allowed to witness the proceedings, a practice that is a carryover from a system in which dispute settlement was viewed as a diplomatic rather than a legal proceeding.[43] In 2005, the United States and the EU showed this could be done by allowing their dispute over compliance with the beef-hormone case to take place in public. Open hearings should become routine. The WTO can stand the light of day and arguments before the panels should all be open to the public. This would contribute to the understanding and acceptance of the system.

Consistency for Authorizations to Retaliate

One of the great achievements of the DSU was the establishment of an Appellate Body. This helps to ensure some consistency across findings. But there is no possibility of appeal when panels authorize retaliation. As a result, there have been some very inconsistent awards of permission to retaliate, particularly with respect to violations of the prohibition on export subsidies, which have their own dispute settlement provisions.[44] In an improved approach, the DSU should be amended so that claimants could be given the option of filing for authorization to retaliate on a contingent basis at the time the original case was brought. The authorization to retaliate could be appealed to the Appellate Body, which would then scrutinize both the findings and the authorization. Later, in the event of noncompliance, the original panel could give final permission for the designated retaliation to be implemented. This change would not only improve the coherence of these awards but might also improve compliance by allowing for speedier retaliation and an increased awareness that retaliation could result from noncompliance.

---

[43] Consultations between the parties could still occur in private, of course.
[44] See Lawrence, *Crimes and Punishments?*, pp. 55–57.

Greater Speed

A particularly problematic feature of the current system is the time it takes for the process to go through all the steps of panel hearings, appeals, and authorizations to suspend concessions. In combination with the fact that there is no retroactivity in authorizations, this gives members an incentive to game the system and delay compliance without consequence. One proposal has been to allow retroactivity in retaliations. But this would mean that retaliation was being used as punishment and exacerbate concerns over the loss of sovereignty. Even if it were only applied from the time the case was initially brought, retroactivity could also result in retaliation that was extremely punitive when infractions are large. Moreover, since retaliation is relatively rare in the first place, the impact might not be very consequential. Alternatively, parties might be required to provide financial compensation or to repay duties that were collected as a result of the violating measure. However, such changes are problematic. As in the case of retroactivity in the retaliation award, they would mean the loss of the presumption that members were acting in good faith, which is an important virtue in an intergovernmental institution. Instead, there is merit in retaining the current system while increasing its resources so that findings can be made more rapidly. This might include funding a stable of panelists that would be available on a full-time basis, and this could be done without changing the text of the agreements.

how else?

CHANGES IN U.S. BEHAVIOR

A Strategic Use of Cases

There are also changes the United States could make in its own use of the system. The first would be to improve its own record of compliance; the second would be to adopt a more strategic approach to cases. Most cases brought by the United States are the result of complaints made by U.S. firms. This is certainly one method for discovering problems, but it should not be the only one. The U.S. government itself could be more active in considering markets with potential for U.S. exports. This might require an improvement

23

in the analytical capacities of the Office of the U.S. Trade Representative (USTR), or perhaps the Department of Commerce. It is striking, for example, that in the first six years of the current dispute settlement system, the United States brought sixty-eight cases; by contrast in the past six years it has brought only sixteen. To be sure, overall the number of cases brought to WTO panels has declined over the two periods, from 219 to 129, but the U.S. decline is much larger. Particularly noteworthy, for example, have been the few cases brought against China despite the very extensive set of complaints published in annual reviews by USTR and despite the fact that cases brought against China have met with some success. The United States has thus far only brought three cases: on Chinese taxes on integrated circuits in 2003, on measures relating to auto parts imports in 2006, and on tax refunds in 2007. China settled the integrated circuits case in 2004, and in March 2007 it announced the repeal of one of the disputed tax measures.

The prescriptions offered in this paper are technical and modest because grand proposals for reform are fundamentally misguided. The dispute settlement system reflects a delicate balance between toughness and respect for sovereignty; rather than criticizing the result, U.S. policymakers and legislators should invest more energy in defending it. And the defense must begin with greater compliance with WTO rulings. America takes unusual care before signing international treaties since it is serious in adhering to its international obligations. Indeed, this care is reflected in the constitutional requirement that treaties require the agreement of two-thirds of the Senate.[45] Yet the U.S. record in WTO cases in which it has been a defendant suggests it has not always been scrupulous in adhering to its WTO obligations. Currently, the United States is actually a defendant in almost twice as many cases as it is a plaintiff, and most WTO cases are won by the plaintiffs.

The U.S. record is particularly poor when it comes to measures adopted to "remedy" supposedly disruptive or unfair behavior by its trading partners.[46] In five of the six times over the past decade that the United States has adopted safeguard provisions (temporary tariffs designed to restrain an exceptional surge in a particular import), these

---

[45] *Constitution of the United States of America*, Art. II, Sec. 2.
[46] See Lewis E. Leibowitz, *Safety Valve or Flash Point?* (Washington, DC: Cato Institute: Center for Trade Policy Studies, 2001).

have been successfully challenged and overturned by U.S. trading partners.[47] Similarly, there have been many losses with respect to the administration of antidumping tariffs (which supposedly punish foreign firms for selling below their cost of production or below the cost at which they sell things in their home market). But the U.S. record of defeat extends beyond the use of these trade "remedies"; U.S. farm policies were found to involve a large number of WTO violations as a result of Brazil's cotton case.[48] In all these instances, the infringements were put in place by government officials or members of Congress, many of whom are actively involved in trade policies. Plainly, compliance with international obligations is not their priority. Given that successful global institutions such as the WTO are both rare and fragile, this attitude is reckless.

Contrary to the complaints of the critics, the fact that the United States has been called to task by WTO panels serves to illustrate their benefits: The dispute settlement system curbs the protectionist instincts of U.S. trade policymakers and so underpins prosperity. But the United States should be complying with WTO rules prospectively, not violating them and waiting for an arbitration panel to play the role of bad cop. Former Senator Bob Dole (R–KS) once advocated a panel to review U.S. defeats in WTO cases and see if the verdicts were justified. But a better role for such a panel would be to explore why the violation occurred in the first place—and to recommend steps to avoid a recurrence. Even if the U.S. record of compliance is better than that of other WTO members, it is in the national interest to comply with rules that improve the performance of the U.S. economy, irrespective of the compliance record of other countries. In the final analysis, good trade agreements provide a country with benefits by making it easier to implement policies at home that boost productivity and competitiveness. Once such policies are established at home, the United States will be in a better position to encourage compliance abroad.

---

[47] When the Bush administration removed its steel tariffs in response to a loss at the WTO, it was the fourth year in a row that the United States had to abandon a safeguard measure approved by the president. Actions on wheat gluten, lamb meat, and line pipe all met a similar fate at the WTO; a broomcorn safeguard was successfully challenged by Mexico under NAFTA Chapter 20. See Robert Z. Lawrence and Nathaniel Stankard, "America's Sorry Trade Performance: Whatever happened to all that talk about the rule of law?" *The International Economy*, Winter 2004.

[48] See Devereaux, et al., *Case Studies in US Trade Negotiation*, Chapter 5.

REFERENCES

Bagwell, Kyle, Petros Mavroidis, and Robert Staiger. "The Case for Auctioning Countermeasures in the WTO." NBER Working Paper No. 9920, 2003.

Bagwell, Kyle and Robert Staiger. *The Economics of the World Trading System.* Cambridge, MA: MIT Press, 2002.

Baily, Martin N. and Robert Z. Lawrence. "Competitiveness and the Assessment of Trade Performance," in Michael Mussa, ed., *Festschrift for C. Fred Bergsten.* Washington, DC: Peterson Institute for International Economics, 2007.

Barfield, Claude E. *Free Trade, Sovereignty, Democracy: The Future of the World Trade Organization.* Washington, DC: AEI Press, 2001.

Bayard, Thomas O. and Kimberly Ann Elliot. *Reciprocity and Retaliation in U.S. Trade Policy.* Washington, DC: Peterson Institute for International Economics, 1994.

Besson, Fabien and Racem Mehdi. "Is the WTO Dispute Settlement System Biased Against Developing Countries? An Empirical Analysis." Paper presented at the Second International Conference on "European and International Political & Economic Affairs," Athens, Greece, May 27–29, 2004.

Bhala, Raj. "The Power of the Past: Towards de Jure Stare Decisis in WTO Adjudication." *George Washington International Law Review*, Vol. 33, Nos. 3 & 4 (2001), pp. 873–978.

Bhala, Raj. "The Myth about Stare Decisis and International Trade Law." *American University International Law Review*, Vol. 12, No. 4 (1999), pp. 845–956.

Bhala, Raj. "The Precedent Setters: De Facto Stare Decisis in WTO Adjudication." *Journal of Transnational Law and Policy*, Vol. 9, No. 1 (1999), pp. 1–151.

Bown, Chad P. "Participation in WTO Dispute Settlement: Complainants, Interested Parties and Free Riders." *World Bank Economic Review*, Vol. 19, No. 2 (2005), pp. 287–310.

Bown, Chad P. "Developing Countries as Plaintiffs and Defendants in GATT/WTO Trade Disputes." *The World Economy,* Vol. 27, No. 1 (2004), pp. 59–80.

Bown, Chad P. "On the Economic Success of GATT/WTO Dispute Settlement." *The Review of Economics and Statistics,* Vol. 86, No. 3 (2004), pp. 811–23.

Bown, Chad P. and Bernard Hoekman. "WTO Dispute Settlement and the Missing Developing Country Cases: Engaging the Private Sector." *Journal of International Economic Law*, Vol. 8, No. 4 (2005), pp. 861–90.

Bradford, Scott C. and Robert Z. Lawrence. *Has Globalization Gone Far Enough?* Washington, DC: Peterson Institute for International Economics, 2004.

Bradford, Scott C., Paul L.E. Grieco, and Gary Clyde Hufbauer. "The Payoff to America from Global Integration," in C. Fred Bergsten, ed., *The United States and the World Economy: Foreign Economic Policy for the Next Decade*. Washington, DC: Peterson Institute for International Economics, 2005.

Breuss, F. "WTO Dispute Settlement from and Economic Perspective: More Failure than Success?" *IEF Working Paper*, No. 39. Vienna, Austria: Research Institute for European Affairs, 2001.

Brimeyer, Benjamin L. "Bananas, Beef and Compliance in the World Trade Organization: The Inability of the WTO Dispute Settlement Process to Achieve Compliance from Superpower Nations." *Minnesota Journal of Global Trade*, Vol. 10, No. 1 (2001), pp. 133–68.

Busch, Marc L. and Eric Reinhardt. "Developing Countries and General Agreement on Tariffs and Trade/World Trade Organization Dispute Settlement." *Journal of World Trade*, Vol. 37, No. 4 (2003), pp. 719–35.

Busch, Marc L. and Eric Reinhardt. "Bargaining in the Shadow of the Law: Early Settlement in GATT/WTO Disputes." *Fordham International Law Journal*, Vol. 24, No.1 (2001), pp. 158–72.

Charnovitz, Steve. "Rethinking WTO Trade Sanctions." *American Journal of International Law,* Vol. 95, No. 4 (2001), pp. 792–832.

Chile and United States. Submission to Negotiations on Improvements and Clarifications of the Dispute Settlement Understanding on Improving Flexibility and Member Control in WTO Dispute Settlement. WTO document TN/DS/W/52. March 2003.

Dam, Kenneth W. *The GATT: Law and International Economic Organization*. Chicago, IL: University of Chicago Press, 1970.

Davey, William J. "The WTO Dispute Settlement System: How Have Developing Countries Fared?" *Illinois Public Law and Legal Theory Research Paper*, No. 05–17 (2005).

Davey, William J. "The WTO Dispute Settlement System: The First Ten Years." *Journal of International Economic Law*, Vol. 8, No. 1 (2005), pp. 17–50.

Devereaux, Charan, Robert Z. Lawrence, and Michael D. Watkins. *Case Studies in US Trade Negotiation, Volume 2: Resolving Disputes*. Washington, DC: Institute for International Economics, 2006.

Ethier, Wilfred. *Punishments and Dispute Settlement in Trade Agreements*. Copenhagen: Economic Policy Research Unit, 2001.

Guzman, Andrew T. and Beth Simmons. "Power Plays and Capacity Constraints: The Selection of Defendants in WTO Disputes." Paper presented at the University of Wisconsin, 2005.

Howse, Robert, and Kalypso Nicolaides. "Legitimacy and Global Governance: Why Constitutionalizaing the WTO Is a Step Too Far" in Roger Porter et al., eds., *Efficiency, Equity, Legitimacy: The Multilateral Trading System at the Millennium*. Washington, DC: The Brookings Institution, pp. 227–49, 2001.

Hudec, Robert. *Enforcing International Trade Law*. Salem, NH: Butterworth Legal Publishers, 1993.

Jackson, John H. "The WTO Dispute Settlement Understanding: Misunderstandings on the Nature of Legal Obligations." *American Journal of International Law*, Vol. 91, No. 2 (1997).

Jackson, John H. "Dispute Settlement and the WTO: Emerging Problems." *Journal of International Economic Law*, Vol. 1, No. 3 (1998), pp. 329–51.

Jackson, John H. "Sovereignty, Subsidiarity, and Separation of Powers: The High-wire Balancing Act of Globalization," in Daniel M.L. Kennedy and James D. Southwick, eds., *The Political Economy of International Trade Law: Essays in Honor of Robert E. Hudec*. New York, NY: Cambridge University Press, 2002.

Jackson, John H. "The Changing Fundamentals of International Law and Ten Years of the WTO." *Journal of International Economic Law*, Vol. 8, No. 1 (2005), pp. 3–15.

Lawrence, Robert Z. *Crimes and Punishments? Retaliation under the WTO*. Washington, DC: Peterson Institute for International Economics, 2003.

Lawrence, Robert Z. and Nathaniel Stankard. "America's Sorry Trade Performance: Whatever happened to all that talk about the rule of law?" *The International Economy* (Winter 2004).

Leibowitz, Lewis E. *Safety Valve or Flash Point?* Washington, DC: Cato Institute: Center for Trade Policy Studies, 2001.

Mavroidis, Petros C. "Remedies in the WTO Legal System: Between a Rock and a Hard Place." *European Journal of International Law*, Vol. 11, No. 4 (2000), pp. 763–814.

Mosoti, Victor. "Africa in the First Decade of WTO Dispute Settlement." *Journal of International Economic Law*, Vol. 9, No. 2 (2006), pp. 427–53.

OECD. "Analysis of Non-tariff Barriers of Concern to Developing Countries." *OECD Trade Policy Working Papers*, No. 16. OECD Publishing, 2005.

Rosendorf, B. Peter, and Helen V. Milner. "The Optimal Design of International Trade Institutions: Uncertainty and Escape." *International Organization*, Vol. 55, No. 4 (2004), pp. 829–57.

Schaffer, Gregory. "Weaknesses and Proposed Improvements to the WTO Dispute Settlement System: An Economic and Market Oriented View." Paper prepared for "WTO at 10: A Look at the Appellate Body," Sao Paulo, May 16–17, 2005.

Schwartz, Warren F. and Alan O. Sykes. "The Economic Structure of Renegotiation and Dispute Resolution in the WTO/GATT System." John M. Olin Law and Economics Working Paper No. 143 (2002).

Wallach, Lori, and Michelle Sforza. *The WTO: Five Years of Reasons to Resist Corporate Globalization*. New York, NY: Seven Stories Press, 1999.

Weiler, J.H.H. "The Rule of Lawyers and the Ethos of Diplomats: Reflections on WTO Dispute Settlement" in Roger B. Porter et al., eds., *Efficiency, Equity, Legitimacy: The Multilateral Trading System at the Millennium*. Washington, DC: Brookings Institution, 2001.

World Trade Organization. *Understanding on Rules and Procedures Governing the Settlement of Disputes*.

APPENDIXES

TABLE 1: EXAMPLES OF FAVORABLE SETTLEMENTS AND RULINGS

IN CASES FILED BY THE UNITED STATES

Case	Defendant	Allegation/Ruling	Outcome
DS309 (2004)	China	The United States contends that China's VAT rebate policy gives domestically produced semiconductors an unfair advantage over foreign producers, in violation of the national treatment principle.	By mutual agreement, China eliminates the availability of VAT refunds on semiconductors produced and sold in China, as well as on those designed in China but manufactured abroad. Semiconductors constitute one of the United States' leading exports to China, amounting to more than US$2 billion.
DS295 (2003)	Mexico	The panel rules that Mexican antidumping duties on beef and rice, as well as various provisions of its antidumping and countervailing duty laws, are contrary to rules on the Antidumping Act (ADA) and the Agreement on Subsidies and Countervailing Measures (SCM).	Mexico revokes antidumping duties on U.S. long-grain white rice. Given that Mexico is the largest export market for U.S. rice, representing over US$800 million of beef and over US$100 million of rice, this presents significant benefits for U.S. farmers.
DS291 (2003)	EU	The EU's de facto moratorium on the approval and marketing of genetically modified organisms (GMO) is found to violate the Agreement on Sanitary and Phytosanitary Measures (SPS), given that such measures are not scientifically justified and lead to undue procedural delays. The WTO ruling also provides that EU measures are not justified by the precautionary principle.	In May 2004, the EU begins authorizing imports of GMOs, purporting to have lifted the moratorium. However, six individual member states still maintained bans for nine GMO products. The U.S. food industry has estimated that the EU moratorium in 1999 and 2003 was costing U.S. producers US$300 million a year in lost sales.
DS245 (2002)	Japan	The panel finds that, because Japanese restrictions on imports of U.S. apples to protect its plants from disease are not founded on sufficient scientific evidence, they violate SPS.	Japan issues a new phytosanitary protocol that complies with the WTO ruling. As a result, U.S. farmers have a new opportunity to export apples to a high-quality export market at a significantly lower cost than before.
DS103 (1997)	Canada	The AB upholds U.S. claims that Canadian export subsidies on dairy products are inconsistent with the Agreement on Agriculture (AoA), and finds that tariff rate quotas (TRQs) for fluid milk imports violate GATT II.	Canada removes its milk TRQs. Regarding export subsidies, a mutual agreement significantly reduces subsidies on butter and an array of milk products. Canada agrees to limit exports to 9,076 tons of subsidized cheese, a quantity equaling less than half of its previous exports.
DS90 (1997)	India	The panel and AB find that India's quantitative restrictions (including prohibitions and import licensing) on a large number of imports violate	India removes an array of nontariff barriers on 2,700 specific products. This granted significant market access to U.S. producers of textiles,

Case	Defendant	Allegation/Ruling	Outcome
		GATT XVIII.	agricultural products, petrochemicals, high-technology products, and other industrial products.
DS36 (1996)	Pakistan	United States claims the absence in Pakistan's laws of patent protection for pharmaceutical and chemical inventions, or of a "mailbox" mechanism for filing patent applications, is in contravention to the Agreement on Trade-Related Aspects of Intellectual Property Rights (TRIPS).	Pursuant to a mutual agreement, Pakistan issues an ordinance with respect to the filing and recognition of patents that brings its national law into conformity with TRIPS obligations and satisfies U.S. concerns.
DS28 (1996)	Japan	United States claims that Japan's copyright regime for the protection of intellectual property in sound recordings is in violation with the TRIPS Agreement.	In a settlement between the parties, Japan passes amendments to its national copyright law to grant full protection for sound recordings retroactively. The U.S. gains from this case are estimated at approximately US$500 million in annual sales.
DS26 (1996)	EC	AB rules in favor of the United States and its co-complainant, Canada, that the EU's import ban on hormone-treated beef is not based on a proper scientific risk assessment and that the scientific evidence provided in support of it is insufficient and fails to comply with SPS.	In 1999, the United States imposes trade sanctions of US$116.8 million against the EU. The EU introduces a new directive addressing bans on the use of hormones in stock farming. In spite of continued disagreement, the EU challenges U.S. sanctions in the first WTO public proceedings.
DS 16, 27, 158 (1995–1996, 1999)	United States with five other Latin American countries	The EU's regime for the importation, sale, and distribution of bananas is found to be inconsistent with GATT, the Import Licensing Agreement, AoA, Trade-Related Investment Measures (TRIMS), and GATS.	In 1999, following dispute settlement body authorization, the United States suspends concessions on nine EU products, amounting to US$191.4 million. A mutual agreement is reached in 2001, in which the EU adopts a new system of banana licenses based on historic reference periods. In 2006, the EU implements a tariff-only scheme.

Source: Compiled from documents from the World Trade Organization, the Office of the United States Trade Representative, and WorldTradeLaw.net.

TABLE 2: EXAMPLES OF RULINGS AGAINST THE UNITED STATES

Case	Defendant	Allegation/Ruling	Outcome
DS311 (2004)	Canada	"Zeroing" and other methodologies used by the United States to determine duties for dumping of Canadian softwood lumber are deemed inconsistent with ADA.	Mutual agreement is reached requiring Canadian regions to levy export taxes. The United States revokes duty orders on lumber and initiates a refund process. Of the US$5 billion the United States has collected since 2002, it agrees to return US$4 billion to Canada.
DS283 (2003)	Antigua and Barbuda	U.S. restrictions on cross-border gambling are found to be inconsistent with its obligations under GATS, including its own Schedule of Specific Commitments.	Congress passes the Internet Gambling Prohibition Act and the Unlawful Internet Gambling Enforcement Act, banning certain forms of online gambling and forcing U.S. financial institutions to block electronic transactions to Internet gambling.*
DS267 (2002)	Brazil	U.S. cotton subsidies and export credit guarantees are found to violate WTO rules on agriculture and subsidies, depressing world market prices in a way that is injurious to Brazil.	United States curtails its export credit guarantee scheme and repeals the "Step 2" subsidy program. Brazil complains that marketing loans and countercyclical payment programs still remain unaltered.*
DS248–9, 251–4, 274 (2002)	EC with eight other WTO Members	U.S. tariffs on steel are found to be inconsistent with GATT XIX and the WTO Safeguards Agreement, given the lack of a causal link between injury and increased imports.	The complainants are allowed to retaliate. EC threatens to impose US$2.2 billion sanctions' worth of U.S. exports, including products from electorally sensitive areas. The United States withdraws safeguards prior to adoption of the AB decision, resolving the dispute.
DS236, 247, 257, 264, 277 (2001–2)	Canada	The panel ruling implies that stumpage fees levied by Canadian provinces constitute a government subsidy and justifies U.S. countervailing duties against softwood lumber exports from Canada. However, the calculation of duties based on U.S. prices is deemed inconsistent with SCM.	In 2006, United States and Canada sign a mutual agreement to manage lumber trade through a series of varying export taxes. Under it, the United States is to return approximately US$5.3 billion it has collected from Canadian companies since 2002.
DS 217 (2000)	EC with seven other WTO Members	The U.S. Continued Dumping and Subsidy Offset Act of 2000 (the "Byrd Amendment") is found to be in violation with ADA and SCM rules.	Given U.S. failure to comply, complainants are allowed to impose sanctions of 72 percent of the amount collected in duties. Canada, the EC, and Japan undertake retaliations. In 2006, the United States enacts the Deficit Reduction Act of 2005, which among other provisions repeals the Byrd Amendment over a two-year transition.

Case	Defendant	Allegation/Ruling	Outcome
DS108 (1997)	EC	The U.S. tax exemption scheme for Foreign Sales Corporations is found to constitute an export subsidy under SCM and to violate the AoA.	EC is granted permission to apply sanctions amounting to over US$4 billion until United States changes policy. In an agreement with the EC, United States passed the Foreign Sales Corporation and Extraterritorial Income Exclusion Act of 2000 into law to stop EC retaliation.
DS2,4 (1995)	Venezuela and Brazil	Environmental Protection Agency (EPA) regulation to reduce the contaminants in gasoline is found to be applied more stringently to foreign refiners than to domestic refiners, in violation of Article 3.	The United States brings EPA regulation to conformity by applying the same standard for domestic and foreign sources of gasoline. This does not require lowering U.S. standards of health and environmental protection, but it does require the nondiscriminatory application of them.

Source: Compiled from documents from the World Trade Organization, the Office of the United States Trade Representative, and WorldTradeLaw.net.

Note: * Denotes that plaintiff has requested a compliance panel due to disagreement between the parties regarding the existence of compliance.

ABOUT THE AUTHOR

Robert Z. Lawrence is the Albert L. Williams Professor of International Trade and Investment at Harvard University's John F. Kennedy School of Government, a senior fellow at the Institute for International Economics, and a research associate at the National Bureau of Economic Research. He served as a member of the President's Council of Economic Advisers from 1998 to 2000. Lawrence has also been a senior fellow at the Brookings Institution. He has taught at Yale University, where he received his PhD in economics. His research focuses on trade policy. He is the author of *A US-Middle East Trade Agreement: A Circle of Opportunity?; Crimes and Punishments? Retaliation under the WTO*; *Regionalism, Multilateralism and Deeper Integration; Single World, Divided Nations*; and *Can America Compete?* He is coauthor of *Has Globalization Gone Far Enough? The Costs of Fragmentation in OECD Markets* (with Scott Bradford); *A Prism on Globalization*; *Globaphobia: Confronting Fears About Open Trade*; *A Vision for the World Economy*; and *Saving Free Trade: A Pragmatic Approach.* Lawrence has served on the advisory boards of the Congressional Budget Office, the Overseas Development Council, and the Presidential Commission on United States-Pacific Trade and Investment Policy.

ADVISORY COMMITTEE FOR

THE UNITED STATES AND THE
WTO DISPUTE SETTLEMENT SYSTEM

Kira M. Alvarez
ELI LILLY AND COMPANY

Raj Bhala
UNIVERSITY OF KANSAS SCHOOL OF
LAW

Barry E. Carter
GEORGETOWN UNIVERSITY LAW
CENTER

Steve Charnovitz
GEORGE WASHINGTON UNIVERSITY
LAW SCHOOL

Christine Elder
U.S. DEPARTMENT OF STATE

Susan G. Esserman
STEPTOE & JOHNSON LLP

Elliot J. Feldman
BAKER & HOSTETLER LLP

Mercedes Carmela Fitchett
CHF INTERNATIONAL

Robert E. Herzstein
MILLER & CHEVALIER

Gary C. Hufbauer
PETER G. PETERSON INSTITUTE FOR
INTERNATIONAL ECONOMICS

Theodore H. Moran
GEORGETOWN UNIVERSITY

Marcus Noland
PETER G. PETERSON INSTITUTE FOR
INTERNATIONAL ECONOMICS

Christina R. Sevilla
OFFICE OF THE U.S. TRADE
REPRESENTATIVE

Shanker Singham
SQUIRE, SANDERS & DEMPSEY, LLP

Bruce Stokes
NATIONAL JOURNAL GROUP, INC.

Sidney Weintraub
CENTER FOR STRATEGIC AND
INTERNATIONAL STUDIES

Phoebe L. Yang
DISCOVERY COMMUNICATIONS, INC.

Note: Council Special Reports reflect the judgments and recommendations of the author(s). They do not necessarily represent the views of members of the advisory committee, whose involvement in no way should be interpreted as an endorsement of the report by either themselves or the organizations with which they are affiliated.

RECENT COUNCIL SPECIAL REPORTS
SPONSORED BY THE COUNCIL ON FOREIGN RELATIONS

Bolivia on the Brink
Eduardo A. Gamarra; CSR No. 24, February 2007
A Center for Preventive Action Report

After the Surge: The Case for U.S. Military Disengagement from Iraq
Steven N. Simon; CSR No. 23, February 2007

Darfur and Beyond: What Is Needed to Prevent Mass Atrocities
Lee Feinstein; CSR No. 22, January 2007

Avoiding Conflict in the Horn of Africa: U.S. Policy Toward Ethiopia and Eritrea
Terrence Lyons; CSR No. 21, December 2006
A Center for Preventive Action Report

Living with Hugo: U.S. Policy Toward Hugo Chávez's Venezuela
Richard Lapper; CSR No. 20, November 2006
A Center for Preventive Action Report

Reforming U.S. Patent Policy: Getting the Incentives Right
Keith E. Maskus; CSR No. 19, November 2006
A Maurice R. Greenberg Center for Geoeconomic Studies Report

Foreign Investment and National Security: Getting the Balance Right
Alan P. Larson, David M. Marchick; CSR No. 18, July 2006
A Maurice R. Greenberg Center for Geoeconomic Studies Report

Challenges for a Postelection Mexico: Issues for U.S. Policy
Pamela K. Starr; CSR No. 17, June 2006 (web-only release) and November 2006

U.S.-India Nuclear Cooperation: A Strategy for Moving Forward
Michael A. Levi and Charles D. Ferguson; CSR No. 16, June 2006

Generating Momentum for a New Era in U.S.-Turkey Relations
Steven A. Cook and Elizabeth Sherwood-Randall; CSR No. 15, June 2006

Peace in Papua: Widening a Window of Opportunity
Blair A. King; CSR No. 14, March 2006
A Center for Preventive Action Report

Neglected Defense: Mobilizing the Private Sector to Support Homeland Security
Stephen E. Flynn and Daniel B. Prieto; CSR No. 13, March 2006

Afghanistan's Uncertain Transition From Turmoil to Normalcy
Barnett R. Rubin; CSR No. 12, March 2006

To purchase a printed copy, call the Brookings Institution Press: 800-537-5487.
Note: Council Special Reports are available to download from the Council's website, CFR.org.
For more information, contact publications@cfr.org